PASSION WAVES
Poetry by Ifi Amadiume

First edition published in Britain 1985
by Karnak House
    300 Westbourne Park Road
    London W11 1EH
    England

ISBN 0 907015 22 0 hb
ISBN 0 907015 23 9 pb

CONTENTS

Some of the poems in this collection have appeared in the following publications:

For Chinelo, Okike, Nigeria
Creation, Okike, Nigeria
Be Brothers, Okike, Nsukka, Nigeria;
Bloody Masculinity, Frontline, London.
Moroko, The Guardian, Lagos, Nigeria.
Bitter, The Guardian. Lagos; *West Africa,* London.

I

PASSION WAVES

PASSION WAVES

My thoughts flow out in waves,
sending shivers through my veins;
my mind is fully charged,
ready to burst of changed
and still changing passion waves.

(FOR SULAIMAN)

My Son
Came into this world
Wrinkles of Wisdom
On his forehead,
Frown deeper than time itself,
Face of an old man
that frightened white people
but made my people wonder
which of the ancient Greats,
in cyclical returns,
is this come back

(FOR NKEMDILIM, MY DAUGHTER)

Nkemdilim, Nkemdilim,
run to me!
Do not stand there
making your cheeks swell out
like two big red tomatoes.
Do not push out your lips
like two red cherries
making figure eight.
Do not turn in your toes
like a duck,
making letter O

Nkemdilim — oo!
run to me, I say,
before I make your bottom red too
like the ripe tomatoes
of your sulky face!

BE BROTHERS

This garment I give you,
let it shield your body,
in return, please shield my baby.

Just as this garment hides your nakedness,
please hide his nakedness and weakness.

This garment I give you,
sown with tender care,
in return, please take care of my baby.

Just as each stitch is sewed with tenderness,
please soothe his sadness and tender tears.

This garment I give you,
one for him, one for you,
in return, please be brothers with my baby.

He comes to you sad,
let him come to be glad,
all for this garment I give you.

(FOR ROSE WHO DIED OF BREAST CANCER AT 38)

She was a beautiful woman,
fresh as the morning rose
still specked in dewdrops.

Comfortable in generous flesh,
she had a heart,
the size of love,
enough for family and friends.

Even more generously full,
a bosom which fed three;
tucked under a nightie
for a night's rest,
it still held the sucking comfort
for a boy three years old,
who soundlessly creeps,
still in sleep,
to a mother's bed,
where tiny hands
will expertly undo
the buttons of separation,
dozily fill the mouth
with pointed roundness
and go back to slumber
in the cushiony warmth
and softness of the breast.

Rounded Rose—
like sisters in millions,
visibly and invisibly consumed—
face to face with deadly,
fast eating,
merciless worms,
claiming the payment of a breast,

lost the race
as she paused to think of
a three year old,
a husband!
not of self!

Between sheets soaking wet
with a weeping woman
and a weeping breast,
the tormenting,
heartbreaking,
ceaseless cry rang,
like the haunting night cry
of the sacrificial victim,
"my breast, my breast!
Please doctor,
I beg you,
do not cut off my breast!"

After all,
the payment?
her breast and her life!

LOVELESS

The goddess of love sits loveless,
her imagination only for company,
knowing her curse is her warmth,
which betrays and destroys.

Alone after lovers leave,
her warmth is her only friend
and the cause of her loneliness.

The woman sits waiting,
to live or to die.

Her warmth, the sap of life
flowing freely in her veins,
giving to others,
taking from her;

it bursts the seeds,
giving to the trees,
but kills the flowers
to give again to others.

(FOR CHINELO)

Had I known Emeka was wooing so ardently,
no way would his love have rivaled mine!
What quantity of love multiplied
could reach mine?

Can he reach into the sky
as I have done
to pluck a love-star
and tuck it in softly in your belly,
as I did three moons now past?

I captured your own wishes in dream.
Last night too,
in gentle sleep,
I delivered the star
six full moons before your time,
sweet sister, child of my mother.

CREATION

Like a sweet orange sucked by a boy,
you have sucked all the goodness out of me.
Still like a boy,
you did not know when to stop.

Like the seed of an orange spat out by a boy,
you have left all the goodness still in me,
still like a boy,
you have left my seed to crop.

I was left naked and unshielded by a boy.
It was not the nakedness of the naked;
it was the nakedness of naked earth;
it was the nakedness of birth;
it was the nakedness of creation.

My seed took root again,
my shield in time regained,
full of sweet juice
again to be sucked.

A LETTER TO YOU

I saw you yesterday.
Perhaps you too saw me
but you would rather touch the meat of dead ox
and cause my wound to open and bleed again.

I came back yesterday
with pain in my heart,
I snapped at my daughter.
She tried to catch some loving in her
own many baby ways
but I was far away
thinking of tears, fever, blood and women.

We could not sleep yesterday.
The baby cried because I was cold
till she came into my bed.
I could not cry for you and reach you
with things in between us,
This morning, I started my menses.

OUR CONTRADICTIONS

My hand
boneless
limply falls,
each time unintended
upon your softness
in response to a pull yet unheeded.

You talk a lot
and burn,
seeking excitement in dim lights,
jazz and marijuana,
still you cannot say,
let's make love.

You take my hands,
gently place them upon your heart
and I see petals sun-bold
ready to enfold a perfect pair.

One step on spiral stairs to paradise,
my senses unfold to tingling touch.
With fire and feelings I thirst;
Oh for a drink of the eternal spring,
tongue and fingers turn antennae,

then like a splash of harsh winter showers,
your words cut through to my bones,
unholy names at sacred times,
how they freeze me!

Stone-cold now,
I resist your timid touch
reaching out in urgent longing,
as I sober and sad
face the bareness of our contradictions.

BLOODY MASCULINITY

Shall I be child of the full moon,
a slave to love
in seasoned womanhood?

Shall I dare worship yet again
starry – eyed in the temple of love
with maidens yet unbroken?

Shall I shed tears of blood
again in loving
while virgins bleed freely,
new initiates in love?

Will the source of my spring
again recede
at the blast of the unbending penis?

Will my womb at the sight of hotness
grow cold and shrink in the face of
bloody masculinity
in this peak of womanhood?

Can I at last
not hope for lingering paddles
in my open waters,
a gentle breeze
to swell my sails
in true pursuit of eternal bliss?

II

SUFI POEMS
(Themes in Islamic Mysticism)

SUFI POEMS (THEMES IN ISLAMIC MYSTICISM)

The seeker/lover, through the state of intoxication *sukr*,
seeks self-annihilation *fana* in knowledge of and union
with the divine essence of the Beloved, *Ma'rifa*, gnosticism.
This type of poetry is rare in Black writing in the West,
but quite common in unpublished manuscripts in local West
African languages such as Hausa and Fula and Wolof, etc., by
those who have been disciples of great Black Shaykhs, saints
and prophets of Sufi tariqas. African influences on both
Islamic and Christian mysticism remains undisputed, yet little
acknowledged.

SEARCHING

Alone in my loneliness at night,
I search for a spot of light,
amidst so much loveliness,
and I in such loneliness,
searching for a spot of light.

Alone in my emptiness at night,
I search for a spot of light;
amidst people so busy,
amidst people so noisy,
searching for a spot of light.

Alone in my search at night,
I search for a spot of light,
never reaching,
ever itching,
searching for a spot of light.

(FOR A SUFI FRIEND)

You lament a friend who died,
a friend you say you liked.

You place him in paradise,
where your good man goes when he dies.

You let him skip one space;
the middle place,
to the highest abode.

Not you, but paradise,
impatient and overjoyed to receive him,

the usual law was set aside,
though by Muslim law he lived.

His death your vacuum;
an end to your life.

You thought you too would die,
for a while, you lived only to sigh;

seeped in emptiness and sorrow,
At last, dry-eyed, you wake up

to remember a friend who died,
put away in paradise,

too high out of reach,
with you below.

Still feet on Earth despised,
you are close to your friend;

earth to earth,
dust to dust.

Do you not remember your friend
in times when beauty is rare and near?

as when you behold the morning star
and all is calm in natural excellence.

Do you not see his gentle eyes in the skies,
soothing and healing yesterday's wounds?

Do you not see him in your imagination,
inspiring words and thoughts you mention?

Much more than all these,
do you not see him in your eyes?

Do you not see him beautiful as flowers,
ready to die, they release many followers,

as their pods break out in seeds?
So are you one of your friend's;

Your friend lives on in full size,
so remember him here, not in paradise.

ALIF

Ali Ali Alif
like infinity.
Ali Ali Alif,
I could love you Ali.
Ali the soft, Ali like Alif,
Alif the infinite.

Ali like Alif,
creeping warmly
under my skin,
travelling to my womb,
Ali Ali Alif,
searching for a soft spot,
a warm nest in me

Ali Ali Alif,
Alif the beautiful,
Alif love,
I could love you Ali.

Ali the tender;
Alif the answer;
Alif the end;
Alif is it,
and I could lose myself,
but let me travel still Alif.

MISTRESS OF MY OWN BEING

Untied of all binding knots—
the tears and ties of time,
freed of haunting memories and regrets,
feelings of contentment rush on
like soft tidal waves,
till slowly, they envelope me.

Thinking of nothing,
wrapped up in my own warmth,
in scents and steam-blankets,
protected in my contentment,
I lie calm and supreme.

In this sweet sanctuary,
I have no need for food or man,
I feel no need for tomorrows,
no need for sound or voices,
only the soothing silence of the night.

Through the dancing folds
of the lacy petticoat of the window,
I see the yellowness of the night;
a huge brilliant eye in heaven
probing me.

In amorous splendour,
she throws out hands full of golden arrows
reaching for the hidden apples
in the folds of my mind.

Not even the sensuality of the moon
can move me now in my calm
Peace and contentment,
let these be my virtue,
as I lie calm and supreme,
Mistress of my own being.

SENSELESS RAPTURE

In longing,
I am without myself;

you hold me
as the sea holds a fish,
with you there is no limit,
without you,
like fish out of water,
I die.

Show mercy in your supremacy,
dilute the strength of wine
in this intoxicating sea,
cool my burning heart,
release gentle dews
onto these swollen lips and cheeks.

Take me
in the brightness of your eyes,
in hues of scattered rubies, pearls and amber.
Take me
in the scent of you steam.
Ravish me completely
and only in your embrace
leave me in senseless rapture.

THE UNION

1.
You stay far far away
and unreachable to me.

Although my soul,
like a baby,
seeks nourishment
in pure flowing nectar
from its mother's bosom,
you go far far away
so unreachable to me.

You stay far away
leaving a lead
weighing heavily
on my gentle soul
which seeks
only to see you.

2.
Tonight,
my love,
as I burn in loving,
I could turn a rat,
cut tunnels,
walk on all fours,
just to reach you.

As I burn in loving,
I could grow wings,
cross the sky,
to reach you.

As I burn like cinder,
I could dissolve
into thin air
just to reach you.

You remain far away,
maddeningly near,
Yet far far away,
so unreachable to me.

3.
Ah one loving embrace,
to end a journey
well begun.
Do not deny,
my love,
this closeness.

To send,
in welcome,
a carpet of colours;
rainbowed spirals;
a path
studded in diamonds;
stones so precious;
a hand full of stars;
and you
at the other end
of brilliantly
lighted ringlets
beckoning on me.

In ripples of laughter,
glided half-way to you,,
before I woke up
like one
gay in ecstasy.

You see,
I know you
even in sleep;
I know you
when you tease;
I know your shadow,
I know your scents,
I know your essence;

Sweet beloved
for that embrace;
the final becoming,
I complete the journey.
Take me now.

4.
Awake,
asleep,
you come to me
fleetingly
like a sweet breeze
I cannot catch
in the palm of my hand.

Awake,
asleep,
I see you
sweet,
serenely haloed
in purity
I cannot hold
in the gaze of my eyes.

Awake,
asleep.
you play on my mind
in such sweet
and gentle tunes,
tingles in my soul
that I cannot caress
with my mortal fingers.

Sweet beloved,
how long now
the final becoming;
when will my soul
cease to hunger.

5.
My love,
my love,
today is unbearable
as my soul
pants in anticipation.

The pain is unsettling
as my heart misses a beat,
thinking its beloved
has come.

Ah for
a gentle touch of wind,
a tiny drop of dew,
one whiff of your scent;

just enough,
my love,
to keep my soul awake
as I await
that final becoming.

6.
(why the veil?)
Do not shroud me
in silk cotton
and shimmery finery;
they,
like my bare flesh,
are of this
transient world—
only fit for worms
from which they were spun.

Leave me open
as I am,
for I do not know
where,
which point of me
the eyes of
my beloved
may rest on

Leave me
as pure as I came
for the final reunion
with my love.

7.
How the eyes of loving
soothe me,
make my flesh burn
with desire
and my blood
jet swift,
clear as a fountain.

Feed, feed,
hungry soul
in the eyes of loving;

tonight, tonight,
the meeting,
the union.

8.
Ah!
to turn the night
into grey,
denying me
the midnight sun!

You sat me
on a moving,
high,
fast,
flying plane
to a faraway place
my fear
refused me to reach.

How in the moment
of danger,
I sought my beloved.
I could not make
the holy sign,
not belonging
to that order;

I only sought you,
called out,
dared pronounce
your sweet name,
my love.

Perhaps tonight,
there will be more courage
to journey
with those unknown
to the brightness
glimpsed
in last night's sleep,
if   only to sight you
sweet sweet beloved,
light of my soul.

9.
Why the generosity
of heart tonight,
the holding,
the squeezing
of hands,
as we burn
in longing
with words unspoken,
eyes luminous,
hands moist,
pain in our hearts.

Still I asked
only for the garment
next to your skin
to wrap me
till the morning dawn;
a gentle sleep
inside a red rose,
scenting you,
dearest my heart.

10.
Secret, secret,
my love!
last night
in sleep,
sweetheart,
I saw
your own beloved
at rest in his tomb.

Ah what curiousity
made me open
the sacred abode.

What compelled
the quickness
of forehead
kissing the holy ground
in supplication.

What jealousy
left your own beloved
a miniature figurine
in a basket,
lid
hurriedly closed
in the quick exit
of an unworthy intruder!

Oh the blindness of love
that would have
none other
except you,
the joy of my heart.

Mercy,
my love,
in tonight's serenade,
let me hear just you,
let me see just you,
let it be just you,
at last,
for the nodal night
of bride and groom.

III

BITTER
VOICE OF THE MASSES

BITTER

If you were to squeeze me and wash,
squeeze me and wash,
squeeze and wash me,
and I foam,
again and again,
like bitter-leaf
left out too long to wither,
you would not squeeze
the bitterness out of me.

NOK LADY IN TERRACOTTA

If I were to write with my blood,
dip deep in the steam of my tears
to tell what sorrow my heart bears,
still I would not have made history,
as I seem not the first to tell my story;

Sad-eyed Nok lady
captured here in this terracotta,
I see reflections in your valley;
that fine deep curve
moulded by the course of sweat-drops
which have run down your brows,
mingled with your tears,
trailing down to leave
the telling marks of time
at the corners of your eyes,
running to the very base of your cheekbones;
delicate, mysterious to the stranger
but special truly to you
Nok lady.

And sad-eyed sisters I see daily,
I know by your looks,
though recorded in no books,
we too have travelled the same road,
carried the same load,
and sipped of the same sorrow;
knowing we are the beginning of
that distant road of long ago —
the very basis; the grass roots —
the mystery and secret of which
locks behind those sad lines
running along the curves
of the eyes of the Nok lady in terracotta.

Sister-tears of denial I share today;
same sap which ran through the mother stem
now runs in her off-shoots and grows on;
once ploughed, she will crop,
though she reaps not what she sows,
for the planters pick her harvest;
pitcher of water, not your water;
land that grows, not your crop;
river-bed carrying not your water;
so mother do you carry their sons
who in turn will marry off your daughters!

Weak-kneed sisters sitting trembling
with nostrils flaring
and that rhythmic shake of the feet,
telling tales of anger and defeat!
He took again without your consent?
Weep not sister, you are not alone,
for you are just one branch of the tree-
The Tree of Life; The Life of Africa;
stretched out across the black land
is that dark mysterious valley
between the legs of Great Mother Nile,
the cradle of our birth
we dare not deny.

Still Mother!
you should not have flirted,
mating with the current
to give birth to civilization,
deserting your children
in your careless amorous trips
between the current and the sun.
Your sons in vengeance,
did they not desert you?
appropriate your daughters?
take control of the lands?
seek alliances exchanging sisters?

Mother!
you were thus left neglected,
those sons left you unprotected,
then the rape began:
persecuting Persians!
merciless Macedonians!
ruling Romans!
ruthless Arabs!
torturing Turks!
treacherous French!
leeche-like English!
You see sister,
the beginning of our anguish.

They too cunningly control lands,
mindlessly exchange sisters,
purposely pass on knowledge
controlling your minds
as you deny yourselves
and refuse to look into her eyes—
the eyes of the Nok lady in terracotta.

2ND WORLD BLACK AND AFRICAN FESTIVAL OF ART AND CULTURE (FESTAC — 1977)

The dot of life
in all its magic
grows, matures
like the seed of plants,
the eggs of fish,
the eggs of birds,
from the female;

so did we all scatter
in diverse ways to many lands,
fathered by all colours,
fed from all cultures.

We suddenly remembered Mother,
the undeniable Mother of Creation;
we all say 'Mother Africa!'
In contingents strong,
we troop back,
retracing lost and old tracks
brothers seeing sisters again,
some for the first time,
for the moment forgetting fathers,
seeing One Mother,
we all say 'Mother Africa!'

All Black — for that is one name,
come back to One Mother,
some to complain of neglect,
some claiming betrayal,
some to seek love, forgiveness,
some to suckle again;
to cure diseases suffered
in cultures strange,
in strength renewed,
to go back and say,

I found again my own,
I have always known my own,
I keep that which is my own,
do not force me to serve your own.
Sisterhood and brotherhood
with that which is our own,
for that which is our own
is our boundary;
it is our strength;
we dare not lose our own,
or we are lost forever,
and forever be strangers, slaves
only in their own.

We will wander far and near,
speak out loud and clear,
but we will never lose sight of
home Mother; Mother Africa,
whose children throng home in periods
to refresh themselves,
settle their quarrels,
eat again from one pot
and re-organize for strength
in the name of Black and African
Festival of Art and Culture.

IVA VALLEY

Man of my mother's people,
in your hair of cotton wool,
I counted strands of wisdom untold.
In your eyes luminous,
I saw pearls
picked by my mother;
a naked beaded maiden
in silky black skin
running wild in Iva Valley.

Man of my mother's people,
in your brows
like garden ridges,
I saw the ancient fruits,
my mother, girlish,
lips cherry black,
eating nuts and berries
of Iva Valley.

Man of my mother's people,
in the strongness of your bones,
your aged body
firm and fatless,
I saw my mother
in lightness of limbs
as drops of water
from a pot
steady on her plaited head
made strings of gems
on her body
sensuous in camwood
as she walked the Iva Valley.

Man of my mothers's people,
today as they put canfor
and perfumes foreign
on my mother''s defrosted body,
as they put my mother
in coffin ghost-white,
man of my mother's people,
as I sought solace
in your sunken eyes
now as cold as the coal-tarred road
that carried my mother far away,
there were no berries
nor precious stones
only broken lorries
and bones of the dead
as we meandered past Milikin-Hill,
sitting oppressive
in dangerous modernity
on Iva Valley
and the heads of the ancient ones,
defiled in rust, petrol and blood.

Man of my mother's people,
they say Iva is like a woman
in incestuous pregnancy
her belly swollen with child;
her own flesh and blood —
her sons,
first Trade Unionists
grounded by the
heavy arms of exploiters
before they could walk,
their bodies,
ridden in white bullets,
were dumped into her,
as they sucked her blackblood,
vampire-like
for coal.

They say the veins of Iva
no longer runs black
but red in blood;
the vampire has sunk its teeth elsewhere,
suckling black blood for oil.

You see,
man of my mother's people,
with stories strong
of roaming restless souls
in Iva Valley,
for fear of ghosts,
they have run round the corner
Nine Miles,
opened the bowels of the Earth
for a new road
to cut off Iva
now in labour.

But ghosts fly!

MAROKO (a shantytown in Lagos — January 1982)

Maroko
in the seat of oil wealth,
to stand in your middle
and shed tears of humiliation!
For want of human dignity,
for want of self-esteem,
for want of respect,
humanity leaves me here forlorn.

Maroko
where alluvial decay
of age-old
disease infested gutters
cement the streets;
where babies suckle by sewage,
eat of rot,
make toys with mud turned green,
where the odour of gutters thick
fouls the air;

where legislators
stop their noses
enroute to a Thousand and Four
furnished flats
stolen from the masses,
videos and Hi - Fi boom,
champagne flows in life high
and beauties make merry
with Honourable Pleasurers,
while Maroko,
yards away,
remains the cage of death,
a human dust-bin
in the seat of Lagos capital.

WE HAVE EVEN LOST OUR TONGUES!

Look,
O heartless ones,
look at our dying people.

There was a time
when for pennies
we filled our bellies;
akara balls,
moimoi,
rolling smoothly
from leaves
fresh and boiled;
beans,
steaming hot,
cooked in spice
and red oil,
fermented maize,
millet,
for porridge.
We broke the night's fast
for pennies!

Look,
O heartless ones,
look at our dying people
today.

The freed wife,
the old woman,
our mothers,
no longer find
grains, seeds, tuber
to cook,
to sell.

No more
the delightful
first morning sight
of schooling children,
running helter skelter,
steaming food bowls,
or black slates
in their hands.

Uniforms still fill the streets,
faces harsh,
eyes restless,
they are armed soldiers,
on the beat,
hungry for anything.

Look,
O heartless rulers,
look at our wretched people
today.

We went to the polls,
we won no respect,
we were losing, losing,
losing everything,
but our mouths.
We could curse them,
we could curse the land,
we could curse the day
they found oil in her

As we grew
more desperate
with hunger and thirst,
embroideries,
fancies
on their shiny brocades,

shimmery silk gowns
grew more elaborate
and bold,
so too
tales of more oil
they sold.

Like mighty dreaded masquerades,
they claimed the streets,
in deed
every decent space
to themselves,
while our people
became glum,
tight lipped
distant spectators
waiting, waiting and waiting.

The soldiers have come,
still we have nothing,
nothing, nothing.
now we have even
lost our tongues,
cut off
by the sharp edges
of khakis
stiffened with the juice
of our grains,
our tubers.

Look,
O heartless dictators,
people are dying, dying,
dying of hunger,
dying of thirst!